THE CREEPING PLAGUE
OF GHASTLY FAÇADISM

London Fruit & Wool Exchange, Spitalfields 2016

THE CREEPING PLAGUE OF GHASTLY FAÇADISM

The Gentle Author

Spitalfields Life
Books

This edition first published in 2019
by Spitalfields Life Books Ltd

1

ISBN: 9780995740167

This book is published with the generous
support of the following readers of
Spitalfields Life:
Clifford & Fiona Atkins, Graham Barker,
Roxy Beaujolais, Iain Boyd, Jill Browne,
Charlie De Wet, Catrin Evans, Keith
Evans, Doreen Fletcher, John Gillman
& Mary Winch, Carolyn Hirst, Terry
Jasper, Stella Herbert, Michael Keating,
Hilda Keen, Pat Lowe, Julia Meadows,
Angus Murray, Jan O'Brien, Delamain
Ogilby Ltd, Society for the Protection of
Ancient Buildings, Penelope Thompson,
Gillian Tindall, Robert Welham, Jane
Williamson, Jill Wilson, and Julian
Woodford.

I am grateful for the assistance of
Rachel Blaylock, Sydney Diack, Walter
Donohue, Lesley Law, Ros Niblett and
Vicky Stewart in the preparation of
my text

The photograph on p.51 is by Pauline
Lord. All other photographs are by
The Gentle Author.

A Spitalfields Life Book
Edited by The Gentle Author

Cover illustration by Thibaud Herem

Designed by David Pearson
Typeset in Adobe Caslon Pro

Printed by Legatoria Editoriale
Giovanni Olivotto Spa
Viale Dell'Industria 2
36100 Vicenza
Italy

Published by
Spitalfields Life Books Ltd
16 Victoria Cottages
Spitalfields
London E1 5AJ

www.spitalfieldslife.com
@thegentleauthor

'The value of these buildings has more than one side, they have many parts, and we are unable to discriminate between the value of one part and another. If we are asked what side of them, what part of them, we want to preserve, we must say our only possibility of preserving them at all is to preserve them whole as they are.'

William Morris, Society for the Protection
of Ancient Buildings 1890

*Façade of Paul Pindar's House, removed from Bishopsgate
to the Victoria & Albert Museum in 1890*

INTRODUCTION

As if I were being poked repeatedly in the eye with a blunt stick, I cannot avoid becoming increasingly aware of a painfully cynical trend in architecture which threatens to turn London into the backlot of an abandoned movie studio.

Façadism is the unfortunate practice of destroying everything apart from the front wall of an old building and constructing a new building behind it. Sticking a new shed inside the husk of a former edifice is a pitiful way to go about things. It is not worthy of the term architecture. If walls could speak, these façades would tell tales of bad compromises and angry developers who, dissatisfied with the meagre notion of repair and reuse, are driven solely by remorseless greed.

Bullied into sacrificing buildings of merit, cowed planning authorities must take consolation in the small mercy of retaining just a façade with the result that architects are humiliated into creating passive-aggressive structures – gross hybrids of conflicted intentions that scream 'Look what you made me do!' in bitter petulant resentment.

As resources grow scarce, the practice of sacrificing good quality buildings for cheapjack disposable replacements cannot be justified because of the wastage and pollution generated by such redevelopment. It is not responsible or sustainable. As the default option, we need to cherish the buildings that we have and apply our ingenuity and imagination to giving them new life, reconfiguring them to serve our evolving requirements.

Yet it is the practice for developers to assume obsolescence of new buildings after a couple of decades according to economic demand, whereas many of the old buildings they destroy were built to last indefinitely. From Spitalfields, I have observed the rise of

I

irregularly-shaped towers in the City of London that are constructed as standardised steel structures on which glass, steel or cast concrete panels are hung to create an exterior surface, making them appear different from each other. These modular façades lack any integration of the inside and outside which you expect of architectural design. Unfortunately, when new buildings are conceived merely as façades then the practice of façading old buildings follows naturally.

The anodyne visual style of these new developments has acquired the description 'spread-sheet architecture' because commonly the elevations literally resemble the columns of accounting software and are constructed to maximise volume and profit at the expense of any other concern. In these degraded circumstances, the architect's task is circumscribed by the imperative to realise the maximum volume as efficiently as possible. Regrettably, the visual style which is the outcome of this reductive utilitarianism has become ubiquitous in the capital in recent years.

Whenever you see an old façade with a new structure behind it, this tells you that a building of distinction and quality once stood there that possessed some degree of legal protection. The compromise which arose was to keep the front wall. The façades that remain stand like tombstones, memorials to distinguished buildings we have lost. None of these façaded buildings should have been destroyed, but this happens because the economic forces driving redevelopment are greater than the legislation to protect what exists already. The recent rise in façadism is a barometer of how far the power balance has shifted away from conservation towards redevelopment. The result has been the loss of too many important and attractive old buildings that once enhanced our city, and their replacement with generic monoliths.

In these circumstances, the reduction of Londoners' quality of life is not quantified. Few who live and work in the city want to see the destruction of our old buildings and the imposition of soulless replacements, yet these choices have been taken out of our hands.

No-one believes the pretence that the original building still exists because the front wall still stands. There are a few examples where an attempt has been made to hide the join but, in my experience, this is a fiction that developers do not strive to maintain. Mostly, retaining the façade is an unwelcome condition of planning permission when the developer's preference would have been complete demolition. Abnegating responsibility, the developer either complains that they were forced to keep the front wall or, occasionally, boasts that they have retained the period features, while the local community grieves that a beloved building and landmark has been destroyed.

Nobody is satisfied. Conservationists blame developers and developers blame conservationists. The national planning system, legislated by central government and enacted by local government, provides both the arena and ground rules for these battles, framing the conflict between adversaries and delivering these disappointing outcomes. The uneasy physical forms of the resulting façaded buildings betray the tensions arising from such compromises and, in this sense, these monsters confront us with the problematic nature of our conflicted society. They become metaphors of the struggle to realise the irreconcilable contradictions of our simultaneous desires for both authenticity and unfettered profit-driven ambition.

Retaining the front wall alone can never be a sufficient compensation for the loss of a building. Even the assumption that it could be raises questionable notions of how we experience the urban landscape. Cynically, it implies we perceive the world as mere surface and it does not matter if what is behind changes, as long as the superficial appearance is preserved. Yet a façade becomes a mask when it conceals a building's change of use – from a philanthropic institution into luxury flats or from a public building into a corporate headquarters – distracting our attention from the reality of the transformation.

Unsurprisingly, architects tend to dislike the requirement of incorporating an existing façade into a new building, which may have been originally conceived in the hope of fulfilling their own design without such compromise. Too often financial subservience overrides self-respect in such cases. No wonder the treatment of the façade is often perfunctory and the resentment is visible. These circumstances explain the strange discontinuities in this hybrid architecture where sometimes a gap is inserted between the façade and the new building, and the architectural styles of the façade and the building behind it are at odds with each other. It is dispiriting when architects pay so little attention to the architectural whole and the rest of us have to live with these abject horrors that confront us only with what we have lost.

This curious phenomenon first came to my attention when I was shown a façaded nineteenth century office building near Smithfield in the nineties. Only the exterior shell had been retained. The developer had increased capacity by replacing high-ceilinged Victorian offices with low-ceilinged modern workspaces. Consequently, the new interior structure did not coincide with the earlier one, which meant that the new floors bisected the old windows.

At the time, it was merely an isolated curiosity. I observed this early indication of a world out of joint with the innocence of an unwitting protagonist in a science fiction drama who ignores the first sign of a warp in reality that will grow to engulf the universe.

The Epicentre of Façadism

Several buildings in my neighbourhood have suffered this fate in recent years, with Spitalfields quickly becoming the epicentre of façadism in London. Confronting these examples daily has become a source of disquiet, leading me to consider the nature and meaning of these curious transformations.

At first in Spitalfields, there was just the façade of the Cock & Hoop public house in Artillery Lane, redeveloped in 2008. Two nineteenth century front walls punctuated by window openings stand at angles to each other, like a book cover propped open. They stand six feet in front of the new building and their windows do not co-incide with the windows behind. Only the steel props which stabilise the façade connect the old and the new.

Although this was a troubling sight, it was the façading of the London Fruit & Wool Exchange in Brushfield Street in the heart of Spitalfields that truly shocked me. It is a textbook example of such an affront. This was a good quality building designed by architect to the City of London, Sydney Perks, in 1927. Originally constructed as a state-of-the-art auction room with a glass roof that simulated sunlight on cloudy days, it was enhanced by wooden parquet floors, careful detailing and significant craft elements throughout. Since the fruit & vegetable market left Spitalfields in 1991, it housed in-numerable small independent local businesses. The destruction of the building was forced through by the Mayor of London against the wishes of the local council and the sole tenant of the new development is an international legal corporation.

Retaining only the frontage of the building with its stone cornice and brick wall, precast panels of 'bricks' and 'stone' were hung on a steel structure erected behind it. These panels of bricks had an artful irregularity designed into them in an attempt to match the tone of the cast 'stone' with the actual stone of the earlier building. Yet these shoddy panels were already becoming chipped and damaged even as they were being put in place.

The loss of the Fruit & Wool Exchange was followed by the destruction of the White Hart in Bishopsgate which traces its origins to 1246. It was replaced with a cylindrical office block rising over the front wall of the ancient tavern. Currently, a dignified block of horse stables to the north of Spitalfields in Quaker Street, constructed by the Great Eastern Railway in 1888, is being reduced to its exterior wall that will contain a new chain hotel. This building was previously occupied by local businesses too.

As I write, British Land is demolishing more than eighty per cent of the fabric of their development site within the Conservation Area in Norton Folgate, a former ancient liberty to the west of Spitalfields. Again, this was forced through contrary to the wishes of the local council who were overruled by the Mayor of London. More than forty separate premises spread across several streets are being reduced to a handful of large corporate offices with floor plates extending across the width of a city block. Only the façades of a few distinctive buildings within this medieval quarter will be preserved as evidence of an urban landscape that developed over centuries. 'A kind of authenticity' is the developer's oxymoronic language to sell this approach. As if there were fifty-seven varieties of authenticity, when 'authentic' is not a relative term – something is either authentic or it is phoney.

And it is far from over. A tall steel tower designed by Sir Norman Foster, which is conceived to erupt from the retained front walls of modest nineteenth century terraces at the corner of Commercial Street and Whitechapel High Street in a Conservation Area, has been submitted to planning.

Now that I am surrounded by façadism on all sides, a certain pattern has become evident. The pressure of the City of London bordering an historic neighbourhood with many old buildings has delivered this rash of inappropriate redevelopment.

Through centuries, Spitalfields evolved as a place outside the walls of the City of London where small trades could benefit from the proximity of wealthy customers while paying cheaper rents for workshops. Yet equally, the City has been an ambivalent influence. It has been a consistent source of violence in the subjugation of its less powerful neighbour and policies enacted in the City commonly have implications in Spitalfields. When Jewish people were forbidden from trading in the City in the twelfth century, they started a market outside the walls which continues to this day as Petticoat Lane Market.

Violence has always had a hand in the creation of the identity of Spitalfields. When Henry VIII 'dissolved' the Priory of St Mary Spital which gives its name to the place, he distributed the properties among his friends and turned the gardens and orchards into his artillery ground. When the Great Eastern Railway cut through across the north of Spitalfields in the eighteen-thirties, thousands were forced from their homes and crowded into nearby streets. It was the same pattern when Commercial Street was cut through in the eighteen-fifties, bisecting the parish from north to south, in order to carry the increased traffic from the docks which the City of London wished to divert from its own streets. And again, when the railway was extended south across the west side of Spitalfields to Liverpool Street, residents were forcibly evicted and their homes demolished.

At the end of the nineteenth century, the construction of Liverpool Street Station entailed the destruction of Paul Pindar's house, a lavish renaissance mansion built to hold the extravagant collections of Queen Elizabeth's envoy to Constantinople, Sir Paul Pindar. The headquarters of the Society for the Protection of Ancient Buildings sits nearby in Spital Square upon the site of the medieval priory and in their archives are letters written in the late nineteenth century by architect C. R. Ashbee pleading with the railway company to save Pindar's mansion. Many of the sentiments and arguments rehearsed in his letters will be familiar to those campaigning today to protect historic buildings from destruction.

In the event, only the frontage of Paul Pindar's house was saved in 1890 and removed to the Victoria & Albert Museum in South Kensington where it sits to this day as a poignant relic, the earliest Spitalfields façade – both a reminder of another time and a strange precursor of things to come. I can only speculate how future generations will view the museum's recent acquisition of a fragment of the frontage of Robin Hood Gardens, an idealistic attempt at social housing in East London in the sixties which has recently been demolished.

The wonder is how Spitalfields has thrived as a working community in spite of the violence enacted upon it – as if an indomitable spirit arose that found its expression in the resourcefulness of the residents of the East End. Yet the generation and maintenance of such a culture relies upon the provision of workshops and housing that are genuinely affordable.

For the most part, the façadism that has been imposed upon Spitalfields in recent years enabled the transformation of buildings which once provided multiple spaces for small local businesses into a handful of large offices for international businesses in the financial industry. The bizarre and awkward appearance of these structures speak of this discontinuity, failing to reconcile elements that do not belong together. In short, the façades of Spitalfields signal the corporate takeover of spaces imposed upon the neighbourhood while maintaining the superficial appearance of continuity of use.

History tells us that Spitalfields is a consistently mutable place where the influence of the wider world always makes itself felt. When Henry VIII's soldiers 'dissolved' the hospital and priory of St Mary Spital, turning out the patients from the infirmary and the Augustinian brothers from the precinct, it must have seemed like the end of days. The world moves on. A century later, the Truman Brewery opened and the Spitalfields Market was established by royal charter, endeavours whose legacies shape the neighbourhood to this day.

There is no doubt that limited resources will increasingly define how buildings are constructed, demanding greater reuse of existing structures and less destruction. London already has examples of buildings that have been façaded more than once. Maybe the façades of Spitalfields will outlive their current forced marriages to find themselves in more sympathetic relationships with buildings yet to be conceived. We can only dream of this future in the hope that our practice of façadism will not endure.

Origins of Façadism

I was always familiar with suburban houses adding porticos to enhance their status, cathedrals adorned by elaborate gothic west fronts and country houses evolving with the fortunes of successive generations through the addition of larger and grander classical façades. Some of the greatest of our cathedrals and country houses are the outcome of this approach to architecture, palimpsests in which the building's evolution can be read by the perceptive viewer. In the past, new frontages were added to old buildings to modernise them or increase their importance. Yet in my time I have witnessed the inverse – the removal of the former building and the retention of the façade.

The origin of façadism lies in the myth of the Potemkin Villages along the banks of the Dnieper River, built to impress Empress Catherine the Great on her visit to the Crimea in 1787 by her former lover Field Marshal Grigory Aleksandrovich Potemkin. Allegedly, painted façades with fires glowing behind were constructed by Potemkin when he was Governor of the region to give the Empress, sitting in her barge, the impression of Russian settlement in contested territory only recently annexed from the Ottoman Empire.

How appropriate that this story is without any convincing provenance and may contain no more reality that the façades it describes. Although this tale was likely invented by Potemkin's political rivals, the legend of the Potemkin Villages has passed into common lore as a means to discuss notions of falsehood, whether architectural or ideological. Yet in the twentieth century, this fiction became a reality as successive authoritarian powers constructed façades to serve their nefarious purposes.

The Theresienstadt concentration camp was used by the Nazis from 1941 as a way-station to the Auschwitz death camp. When the

Danish Red Cross insisted on an inspection in 1944, façades of shops, a cafe and a school were constructed as part of a beautification programme which succeeded in convincing the inspectors that nothing was amiss.

During the fifties, North Korea built Kijongdong as a model village designed to be seen from across the border in South Korea. The propaganda message was that this was an affluent settlement with a collective farm, good quality housing, schools and a hospital, but the reality was that these buildings were empty concrete shells in which automated lights went on and off.

In a strange enactment of the Potemkin Villages, when Vladimir Putin visited Suzdal in 2013, derelict buildings were covered with digitally-printed hoardings showing newly-built offices of glass and steel. Similar printed hoardings are often to be seen in London with images of the buildings behind, sheltering them from public view while the practice of façadism is underway.

You might conclude that these grim authoritarian precedents would discredit façadism as an acceptable practice entirely, yet it was legitimised by postmodernism at the end of last century. Irony and discontinuity were defining qualities of postmodern architecture, permitting architects to play games with façades and fragments of façades without any imperative to deliver an architectural unity. The ubiquitous façadism of today is the direct legacy of this movement, except now it is enacted without inverted commas and licensed as orthodox in the vocabulary of contemporary architecture.

On Photographing Façades

One day I was walking through Crispin Street in Spitalfields, when the gates in the hoardings surrounding the redevelopment of the Fruit & Wool Exchange swung open to reveal an astonishing vista with the rear of the façade stretching away to the east where it met

Nicholas Hawksmoor's Christ Church. By chance, I had my camera with me and I was able to able to photograph this extraordinary vision that had been granted.

When I studied this picture later, I was fascinated by the similarities with eighteenth century engravings of classical ruins, even down to the artfully placed figure in the foreground to give a sense of scale. In such images, the ruin is commonly either the relic of a distant age or the casualty of a war that destroyed a civilisation. The ruin in my photograph is neither of these, although it is the outcome of institutionalised violence. I find it grotesque – a relic of a recent building of integrity juxtaposed with Hawksmoor's architectural masterpiece, as part of the process of the construction of a generic corporate block.

Gripped by the contradictions in this picture, I began photographing other façades that I encountered in the city. Some I sought out and others I came across. When I published these pictures online, the response was enormous and I learnt that a great many people shared my horror and amazement at these curious spectacles appearing in our streets.

As a result, I was invited to give an illustrated lecture at the Royal Institute of British Architects in which the pictures drew an equal mixture of laughter and revulsion. This was followed by an article for The Architectural Review accompanied by a gallery of London façades in an issue devoted to architects around the world who were working with old buildings to give them new life in creative and sympathetic ways rather merely façading them.

When I googled London façadism, I discovered that a great many of the images were mine and that, in many cases, I alone had captured the moment after demolition and before construction when only the front wall was standing. Recognising the power of these images in drawing strong emotional responses, I realised that a book of them would be an effective means to draw attention to the objectionable practice of façadism and the destruction of good buildings that it conceals.

I am grateful to the readers of Spitalfields Life who alerted me to examples of façadism across the capital, sending me on 'façade safaris' in the summer of 2019 to compile this collection of trophy specimens. This photographic quest took on its own life and I must confess I sometimes took guilty delight in discovering those bizarre examples which offered the most photogenic possibilities.

Evidently, when the discussion takes place between developers, architects, planners and conservationists a certain nuance enters the debate too. It is in the nature of human beings to seek compromise when negotiating. The questions arise – 'Surely it is better to keep the façade at least?' versus 'What is the point in keeping just the façade, why not get rid of the old building entirely?' Yet this is looking at the question from the wrong direction. The real question that should be asked is 'What is the point in keeping just the façade, why not simply keep the whole building?'

I hope my pictures clarify this debate by demonstrating how wrong the practice of façadism is and how, in each case, the original building should never have been destroyed. I defy anyone to look at this gallery of notorious façades and not be appalled.

Why Façadism is Happening

London is a city that has evolved through waves of redevelopment, often after catastrophes such the Great Fire and the Blitz. In this century, we have seen a new wave of development driven by overseas investment, reflecting London's status as a global metropolis and the willingness of our city fathers to accept overseas investment without asking too many questions.

Our government chooses to encourage the development and construction industries by zero-rating new construction for VAT, whereas the renovation or repair of existing buildings is taxed. Thus the destruction of old buildings is incentivised financially, while the reuse and repurposing of buildings is discouraged. This irresponsible policy is directly in opposition to environmental concerns and reflects a preference for short-term economic gain regardless of long-term consequences.

In this sense, the destruction of our heritage is government policy. It has been very disappointing to witness how Historic England, the government's heritage agency, has been on the wrong side of too many important London planning battles in recent years, advocating – or at least making no objection to – the destruction of Smithfield General Market, the historic terrace at Kings College in the Strand, the Marquis of Lansdowne in Dalston and Norton Folgate in Spitalfields, as well as the loss of the Whitechapel Bell Foundry as a working foundry.

Over recent decades, traditional centres of affluence in the capital such as the City of London and the West End have expanded into neighbouring areas such as Spitalfields, Soho and Southwark, characterised by the presence of old buildings and designated as Conservation Areas. Almost all the buildings featured in this book are in these areas.

In Conservation Areas, developers come up against restrictions upon redevelopment yet the escalating land values make them attractive propositions for new buildings. When developers acquire sites in these areas, they hope to demolish the old buildings in order to build the largest new buildings possible, but they come against resistance. Conservations Areas extend a degree of protection to the buildings within their boundaries, and historical significance or listed status can lead to development proposals being rejected by local councils.

When this happens, developers can appeal to the government's Planning Inspectorate or lobby the Mayor of London or the Secretary of State to overturn the decision. Mostly, a compromise is sought. The council insists that the façade of the building must be retained and this option is backed by the government, who permit a new development to be zero-rated for VAT if retention of the façade is a condition of planning permission granted by the local authority. Thus the government's legislative structure supports the practice of façadism just as the intricate cages of steel girders support the façades in this book.

What Façadism Means

From the moment in 2016 when the gate swung open and the façade of the London Fruit & Wool Exchange was revealed to me, my understanding and knowledge of façadism has grown. As the protagonist in the science fiction drama who first encountered a small sign that the world was out of joint, nearly thirty years later I have reached the climax where the curious phenomena surround me. Everywhere I go, I see façades.

These have been years of accelerating development in the capital, with old buildings vanishing and new buildings appearing as the city transforms before our eyes. This environment has allowed the creeping plague of ghastly façadism to spread almost invisibly across the capital, while the attention of the populace has been distracted by the exotic new buildings emerging on the skyline. By their nature, these subtle reconfigurations are less visible than the more obvious visual changes even if the implications are no less significant.

When the façade of a building is preserved, there is a sense that the reality of the change of use of the site is denied, even if the mutation of the building is obvious.

The prevalence of façadism has coincided with the growth of digital culture and our fascination with the virtual as an alternative to the temporal world. Of the people in my photographs, those that have mobile devices are not paying any attention to the buildings or the world around them. We delight to curate our social media with attractive images of ourselves, our friends and our pastimes, without regard to whether or not this is a true picture of our lives.

In all societies, it is the purpose of culture to mediate between appearance and reality. It suits us not to look too closely at the world around us and exist within a narcissistic bubble, ignoring inconsistencies and believing half truths. This book is written at a strange moment when the most successful politicians are also the biggest liars. When old buildings speak to us, they tell troubling stories of past aspirations, of deprivation and of struggle, of industry and of privilege. I can understand how for many people, it is simpler to live with the surface of history and to ignore the changes that are happening around us in the present day. Façadism suits us very well, it is our 'kind of authenticity.'

PLATES

College East, Toynbee Hall, Wentworth Street, Spitalfields, E1

This was part of the Toynbee Hall campus designed by Elijah Hoole and built between 1884–5. It was demolished and façaded for the construction of Attlee House which was completed in 1971. This was demolished in 2016, apart from the façade of College East which has been retained on the front of a new development of flats for the commercial market.

Toynbee Hall was founded in 1883 by social reformer Canon Barnett, vicar of St Jude's Spitalfields, and his wife Henrietta Barnett in memory of Arnold Toynbee, an economic historian. In the eighteen-seventies, Toynbee recognised that the free market system always disadvantaged the poor. He came to the East End from Oxford to work in the creation of trade unions and public libraries, as a means to give practical expression to his social beliefs, but burnt out and died at the age of thirty in 1883.

Attlee House was named after Clement Attlee, secretary of Toynbee Hall from 1909. In 1919, he became Mayor of Stepney, then MP for Limehouse in 1922 and leader of the Labour Party in 1935. Appointed Prime Minister in 1945, Attlee is remembered as the architect of the Welfare State.

12–13 Greek Street, Soho, W1

Built *c.*1683, this was originally the largest house in the street and known as Portland House. From 1774–97, it was Josiah Wedgwood's London warehouse, showroom and enamelling rooms with five showrooms on two floors, where a famous dinner service made for the Empress Catherine of Russia was displayed in July 1774. Repairs were carried out in 1786 by T. Freeman of Great Pulteney Street who made a valuation of the fixtures in 1790 – listing a hall, a counting house and a shop on the ground floor, and a great room, another room, a flowerpot room and a gallery on the first floor.

52–58 St Giles High Street, Covent Garden, WC2

This façade was constructed at the end of the nineteenth century to unify a row of existing houses and shops, which were extended on their upper floors to create a block of mansion flats.

The Post Office directory for 1882 lists Robert Barwell, builder at 52, William Browne, a la mode beef shop at 53, Francis Lebeau, dining rooms at 54, Henry Morrell tobacconist at 55, Martha Peck, ham dealer at 56, Henry William Disley, printer at 57 and William David Fowke, tobacco manufacturer at 58.

By 1910, Richard Maynard, music seller is at 52, Ernest C. Rolls & Co, theatrical revue producers are at 53, Salisbury House mansion block is at 54, Standard Feature Film Company Ltd is at 55, Winchester House mansion block is at 57 and Atlas Electrical Company is at 58.

Creed Court, 3–5 Ludgate Hill,
City of London, EC4

The Victorian office building behind this 1885 painted stucco frontage was demolished in 1985 and replaced by another building that has itself now been demolished to construct a new hotel behind the original façade.

Silwex House, 1–9 Quaker Street, Spitalfields, E1

Silwex House was built between 1873–94 as stables for the Great Eastern Railway. The building extends down to the railway line at the rear with large lifts designed to carry several workhorses at a time. When it was no longer in use as a stable, Silwex House served as premises for small businesses, notably as a textile warehouse. Largely unchanged since it was first built, most of the original features – including the stalls and lifts – were there until it was destroyed in 2018.

55–91 Knightsbridge, SW1

Ecclesiastical architect William Douglas Caroe designed this elaborate Grade II listed terrace for the Church Commissioners in 1902. It is adorned with busts of notables of the day.

Between 28th September and 3rd October 1975, the Spaghetti House siege took place at 77 Knightsbridge. After a robbery went wrong, three gunmen barricaded themselves into the restaurant, taking the staff hostage. All the staff were released unharmed after six days, when two of the gunmen gave themselves up and the leader shot himself.

Royal Arsenal Co-operative Society,
180–214 Upper Tooting Road, Tooting, SW17

This large department store of 1923 with its fine art deco tiled frontage was once the pride of Tooting.

Former American Embassy,
30 Grosvenor Square, Mayfair, W1

The American Embassy London Chancery Building was designed by Finnish-American architect Eero Saarinen and constructed in the late fifties, opening in 1960. A gilded aluminium eagle by Theodore Roszak, perched on the roof with a wingspan of thirty-five feet, distinguishes this London landmark.

The building has nine storeys, of which three are below ground. Grade II listed, it is considered to be a classic of modern architecture in the twentieth century.

The United States paid a peppercorn rent to the Duke of Westminster for use of the land and, in response to an American offer to buy the site outright, the Duke requested the return of his land confiscated after the American Revolutionary War, namely the city of Miami.

Only the façade of Eero Saarinen's building stands now, pending redevelopment as a luxury hotel.

Empire Cinema, 56–61 New Broadway, Ealing, W5

The Empire Cinema was designed by John Stanley Beard in an Italian Renaissance style. It was one of a pair of near identical theatres which were built by Beard for Herbert Yapp in 1934. The other was in Kentish Town and both were taken over by Associated British Cinemas (ABC) within a year of opening. Each had façades dominated by eight tall columns with a double row of windows between the inner six, and seated 2,175 people on two levels. The Empire closed in 2008 and was demolished in 2009 when the doors were installed in its counterpart in Kentish Town to replace ones lost over the years.

Buckingham Gate, Westminster, SW1

This terrace of Grade II listed town houses opposite Buckingham Palace was probably designed by Sir James Pennethorne, *c.*1850–55. They are faced in stucco with Italianate details, comprising four tall storeys plus basements and dormered mansards. Each house is three windows wide with large Doric columned porticos and recessed plate glass sashes.

Stafford Mansions, Stafford Place, Westminster, SW1

This elaborately styled mansion block of 1898 was constructed of bright red rubbed brick and stone banding, with bay windows, high-pitched slate roofs and pedimented gables. Situated at the rear of Buckingham Gate which was in the previous photograph, it is now reduced to a façade and subsumed within a larger redevelopment that engulfs the entire block.

St Bartholomew's Hospital, Smithfield, City of London, EC1

Hospital surveyor, E. B. I'Anson's Pathology Block of 1907–9 derives its style from James Gibbs' designs for the courtyard of St Bartholomew built between 1730–68.

Originally founded by Henry I's jester Rahere in 1123, Barts is Britain's oldest hospital still operating from its original site. It was refounded by Henry VIII in 1546, in an agreement granting the hospital to the Corporation the City of London and described as the 'House of the Poore in Farringdon in the suburbs of the City of London of Henry VIII's Foundation.'

In 1993, Barts was recommended for closure and the Accident & Emergency Department shut in 1995, but in recent years it has developed as a centre of excellence in cardiac and cancer care.

I'Anson's Pathology Block is being redeveloped by Nuffield Health as a forty-eight bed private hospital.

191–199 Archway Road, Highgate, N6

Built in the nineteenth century as 'Richardson of Highgate,' furniture dealers, with flats to house the staff above, and workshops and stables for delivery horses at the rear. In recent years, these workshops were home to over thirty small businesses.

43

19 Hurst Avenue, Highgate, N6

One of a symmetrical pair of semi-detached double-fronted thirties suburban dwellings of two storeys with full height canted bay windows, parapets and shallow sloping tiled roofs. Their façades are unadorned except for white painted timber door surrounds and hoods. Both houses retained their original sash windows and were considered to make a positive contribution to the Crouch End Conservation Area in 2010.

18 Broadwick Street, Soho, W1

Decorative brick inlay on the Berwick Street elevation declares this was constructed in 1886.

Originally a bakery, it became Central Chemists in 1950 when the ground floor and basement premises were acquired by Gertrude Kramer. Michael Moss acquired the pharmacy and freehold to the building from Mrs Kramer in the seventies and he enlarged the shop to include 85–86 Berwick Street in the late eighties, naming it Broadwick Pharmacy. Richard Piercy bought the shop in 1990 and ran it as Zest Pharmacy until 2016.

In recent memory, the upper parts of the building were used as offices by music, film and voice-over businesses.

Broadwick Street (formerly Broad Street) is celebrated as the birthplace of William Blake and notorious for the outbreak of cholera in 1854 which killed over six hundred people before the origin was traced by Dr John Snow to the water pump on the corner of Lexington Street.

47

Thames House, 18 Park Street, Southwark, SE1

Included on the 1872 Ordnance Survey map, the architectural style of Thames House with its gables and gothic details suggest it was built, after construction of the 1866 railway viaduct nearby, in the early eighteen-seventies when this style became fashionable. The 1966 Goad Map shows Thames House occupied by Brooke Bond Tea warehouse and packing.

Abbey House, 219–229 Baker Street, Marylebone, NW1

This impressive towering art deco edifice was originally constructed as the headquarters of the Abbey Building Society in 1932. It was demolished apart from the façade and tower in the seventies, and then demolished again apart from the façade and tower in 2005, when Abbey National moved out and it was rebuilt as flats.

In 1887 when Sir Arthur Conan Doyle invented an address for Sherlock Holmes, he deliberately chose 221B Baker Street because it did not exist, but when Abbey House was built in 1932 as 219–229 Baker Street, it came into existence. Almost immediately after Abbey House opened, letters began arriving addressed to Professor Holmes and for many years the building society employed a writer to compose appropriate replies.

47 Bartholomew Close, Smithfield, City of London, EC1

This narrow four storey frontage was designed by Sir Aston Webb in brick with white rendered detailing. The elevation comprises a slender canted bay on the first floor and above, with a single window and entrance bay to the side. The lintel over the entrance is dated 1910 AD. In 1938, this was Evans Sons Lescher & Webb's salt store and in 1958 listed as GPO telephone offices.

Pyke's Cinematograph Theatre, 56 Shepherds Bush Green, W12

Impresario Montague Pyke opened the Shepherds Bush Cinematograph Theatre on 3rd March 1910 and it showed films until 1981, when it closed with *The Fog*. In 1923, after Pyke went bankrupt, it was reconfigured by John Stanley Beard as the New Palladium, becoming subsequently the Palladium, the Essoldo, the Classic, and finally Odeon 2. Despite surviving a flying bomb, a period of dereliction and a decade as the Walkabout Australian Bar, it was demolished in 2019 and is destined to serve as a façade on a hotel tower.

80 Grosvenor Street, Mayfair, W1

Built in 1852–3 to a design by Sydney Smirke, a prolific architect who is best remembered for the circular reading room at the British Museum.

40–42 Oxford Street, W1

Designed by architects R. H. Kerr & Son in 1923, converted into a bank by architects Palmer & Holden in 1931, and considered to be a building of merit in the Hanway Street Conservation Area.

Lees Place, Mayfair, W1

This is a fragment of the mews attached to 22–23 Grosvenor Square and 43 North Audley Street which was constructed as a single, vast mansion in 1906, designed by Read & Macdonald on behalf of Holloway Brothers developers, who spent £25,000 on the house and paid a rent of £650 to the freeholder, the Duke of Westminster.

Faced with Portland stone, the mansion boasted a spacious hall and staircase, large interconnecting chambers on the main floors and a musicians' gallery. Unable to sell the house, Holloway Brothers let it from 1909–12 to the American banking magnate A. J. Drexel, who commissioned improvements from Sir Charles Allom including an enlarged ballroom 'entirely Louis XVI in decoration' and installed marble floors and staircases.

In 1931, the building was divided up into flats and then heavily reconstructed after bomb damage in the Second World War. Now it is just a shell.

6 Palace Court, Bayswater Road, Hyde Park, W2

Dating from 1892, this elegant mansion facing Hyde Park was designed by Carlos Edward Arthur Ryder in the style of the Aesthetic Movement and built by Holloway Brothers. It comprised four storeys plus mansard roof with gable pitched dormers, and a chamfered bay and arched recessed third floor, with attractive terracotta window dressings throughout.

National Provincial Bank, Threadneedle Street, City of London, EC2

The National Provincial Bank of England on the corner of Thread-needle Street and Bishopsgate was designed by John Gibson as London's largest banking hall. It was constructed in 1863–5 and in 1878 figures were added along the roof line that represent cities where the bank did business including Manchester, Birmingham, Dover, Newcastle and London. Above the arched windows, eight sculpted panels of heroic allegorical scenes represent the achievements of mankind: The Arts, Commerce, Science, Manufacturing, Agriculture, Navigation, Shipbuilding and Mining. It is Grade I listed.

The Cock & Hoop, Artillery Lane, Spitalfields, E1

Thomas Lloyd is recorded as the first landlord in 1805. Victualler Nathaniel Gill married Maria Elizabeth Bradbrook, a baker from Bethnal Green, in 1849 and died a few months after their marriage. Maria took over managing the pub and started the Cock & Hoop Ragged School there, employing William Wright as master. The pub was renamed The Artillery Tavern in 1873 and may have been rebuilt at this time, closing for good in 1908.

Then the building was incorporated as additional accommodation for the Providence Row Night Refuge & Convent which faced onto the next street, Crispin Street. In 1982, it was described as Pursell House, 'hostels for working girls.'

The Providence Row Night Shelter which had opened in 1867 closed in 2002 and, after reconfiguration, was converted into student housing for the London School of Economics in 2006.

465 Caledonian Road, Islington, N7

Mallett, Porter & Dowd constructed this modest yet handsome utilitarian building for their warehousing, storage and removals business in 1874.

Redevelopment by University College London for student housing was turned down by Islington Council in 2010, citing 'adverse visual impact' and inadequate daylight, due to the windows of the new building not aligning with those in the façade. This judgement was overturned by the government's Planning Inspectorate on the basis that 'due to intensive daytime activities taking place at the university campus,' the absence of both light and view 'would not be unacceptably oppressive.'

The development was winner of Building Design's Carbuncle Cup for 2013.

Union Hall, Union Street, Southwark, SE1

In 1782, the Union Hall was built as the Surrey Magistrates Court, which had previously sat at the Town Hall in Borough High Street. It was façaded for offices in 2005.

60 Holborn Viaduct, Holborn, EC1

This office block of 2014 for Amazon includes a reconstruction of William Haywood's northern pavilion, one of four, providing pedestrian access to and from Farringdon Street at each corner of Holborn Viaduct. Originally constructed between 1863 and 1869, it was London's first flyover.

Four statues on the parapets represent Commerce and Agriculture on the south side, both by sculptor Henry Bursill, and Science and Fine Art on the north side, by Farmer & Brindley Architectural Sculptors.

In the Blitz of 1941, both the northern buildings were destroyed, but with this eastern pavilion reconstructed and the western pavilion replaced in 2000, Holborn Viaduct stands intact again.

213 Borough High Street, Southwark, SE1

Only the crown motif visible on the parapet reveals that this was once the Crown public house, with the earliest landlord recorded as Thomas Fleming, wine and brandy merchant, in 1817. The notorious poisoner George Chapman was briefly landlord here in 1902, which may explain the change of name to the St George Distillery public house in the census of 1911.

Kops Brewery, Townmead Road, Fulham, SW6

Kops, founded by Henry Lowenfeld, was the first brewer of non-alcoholic beer in the United Kingdom, constructing an eight acre brewery on Fulham Wharf for ales and stouts in 1890.

Lowenfeld was a Polish-born entrepreneur and theatrical impresario, who built the Apollo Theatre in London and a luxury hotel in Sandown on the Isle of Wight as well as Kops Brewery.

Kops flourished with the rise of the temperance movement, exporting to America during prohibition and throughout the British Empire. As the temperance movement lost influence, the fortunes of the brewery went into decline. Yet Lowenfeld, who left Poland in the eighteen-eighties with ten dollars in his pocket, was able to buy himself a large estate in his country of origin.

Union Wharf, 317 Kingsland Road, Dalston, E8

The first tenants of Union Wharf were the coal merchants, Reeves & Briggs in 1822, who moved in upon completion of the Regents Canal.

In the eighteen seventies, the wharf was acquired by Thomas Blyth, a cement and lime merchant who remodelled the stables, hayloft and granary, adding an ornate office building and boundary wall built with visibility in mind, facing onto the Kingsland Road.

The piers each have chamfered and recessed panels, acanthus leaf decoration below the capitals and a moulded string at head height. They are each capped by shaped turrets or caps with pear-shaped finials to the outer piers.

The central bay is wider than the two flanking bays and incorporates a large double width window. The window sills are built level with a step out wall plinth and the window openings incorporate prominent stucco surrounds, depressed heads and feature keystones.

This is now the Hackney New School, a mixed-ability secondary school focused on music.

Whitechapel Public Baths,
25 Old Castle Street, Spitalfields, E1

Following Edwin Chadwick's sanitary report of 1842, a Committee for Baths for the Labouring Classes was formed in October 1844, spurred on by concern to prevent further outbreaks of cholera. The Committee agreed to make their first intervention in Whitechapel and subscriptions were sought.

Inspired by the 1846 Baths & Washhouses Act, this pioneering facility where people could wash themselves and their laundry was designed by Price Pritchard Baly and completed in 1851. Its construction was utilitarian, combining brown brick walls with an iron roof. The Builder lauded its 'useful' design but described the scheme as entirely devoid of the 'beautiful,' noting that its appearance was 'not simply plain and unpretending, but downright ugly.'

Lack of funding forced the Committee to abandon its ambition to build four bathhouses of several storeys each and the single storey Whitechapel Baths was their only success.

The bathhouse closed in the nineteen-nineties and was rebuilt as the Women's Library in 2002. Since 2013, it has become an events space for London Metropolitan University.

Spiegelhalter Brothers, 81 Mile End Road, Stepney, E1

Georg Spiegelhalter opened his watch and clockmaker and jeweller's shop in Whitechapel at 6 Mount Place in 1828 after he emigrated from Neukirch, Germany. His son Otto moved the business to 81 Mile End Road in 1892. Otto had fifteen children and, when he died in 1902, the shop was taken over by his sons – the Spiegelhalter brothers, Edward, Emil, Leo, Frank & George – who had been born on the premises.

Built in 1927, Wickhams Department Store in the Mile End Road aspired to be the 'Harrods of East London.' The developers assumed the small shopkeepers in the terrace would all fall into line and agree to move out so their new store could proceed. But they met their match in Leo Spiegelhalter who refused and the characterful old shop famously remained sandwiched in the middle of the generic neo-classical department store even after Wickhams closed in the sixties.

George's son Michael Spiegelhalter continued in the shop until 1988 and the elaborate nineteenth century frontage with its curved glass and mosaic survived until recently.

The planning application to redevelop the department store as offices claimed 'the attractiveness and uniformity of 69–89 Mile End Road is only marred by 81 Mile End Road which is inferior in terms of appearance, detailing and architecture.' Yet Spiegelhalters was described by Ian Nairn as 'one of the best visual jokes in London' and, after a public outcry, the developers were forced to keep the Spiegelhalters façade, rather than adopt their preferred option of an architectural void.

Wellington House, 133–155 Waterloo Road, Waterloo, SE1

This was built in 1928 by Payne Wyatt as headquarters for the David Greig grocery chain. In 1979, it was demolished apart from the Ionic-columned façade which is Grade II listed.

Green Arbour House, 16–17 Old Bailey, City of London, EC4

Green Arbour House was designed in 1912 by Arthur Usher of Yetts, Sturdy & Usher in the Edwardian Baroque style for the London, Chatham & Dover Railway Co and built of Portland stone with a Westmorland slate roof.

The major part of the ground floor, together with a portion of the basement and first floors, were used by the parcels department of the railway company with the upper floors devoted to offices.

It is Grade II listed.

Coutts Bank, 440 Strand, Charing Cross, WC2

Architect John Nash designed the West Strand Improvements, constructed in 1830 by William Herbert, which included 449 Strand with its diagonally-placed pepperpot towers.

In 1904, Coutts Bank moved into 440 Strand. They employed Sir Frederick Gibberd, architect of Liverpool Cathedral, to redevelop the entire block between 1974 and 1978, creating a vast modern banking atrium behind the skin of Nash's terrace.

Bartholomew Close, Smithfield, City of London, EC1

The meeting of the old and new in Bartholomew Close.

Part of former Middlesex Hospital, Riding House St, Fitzrovia, W1

The Middlesex Infirmary 'for the Sick and Lame of Soho' opened in 1745, moving to purpose-built premises in Marylebone Fields in 1757. Over the next two centuries, the Hospital expanded to fill an entire block, absorbing other buildings and extending into surrounding streets.

In 1747, it became the first Hospital to provide lying-in beds for pregnant women and, in 1796, the Hospital opened a ward for sick French clergy who were refugees from the Revolution.

Florence Nightingale worked at the Hospital when it was overwhelmed during the cholera outbreak of 1854. In 1987, the Broderip and Charles Bell Wards became the first dedicated to the care of patients with AIDS and HIV-related illnesses.

When the Middlesex Hospital closed in 2006, services moved to the newly built University College Hospital and most of the building was demolished in 2008, apart from a few façades and the Grade II listed chapel in Italian Gothic style.

Maltina Bakery, Valentine Place, Waterloo, SE1

This was constructed in 1907 for Maltina Bakeries of stock brick and faience with neo-classical elements. The Albion Flour Mill had been established nearby in the seventeen-eighties and the Blackfriars Flour Mill in the the eighteen-eighties. These, along with the founding of the British National Bakery School in 1884, marked the beginning of a long tradition of baking in the area which persisted until the late twentieth century.

Despite the Maltina Bakery being identified as a building of merit in the Valentine Place Conservation Area in 2012, permission was granted in 2015 to demolish all but the façade, sacrificing the building's distinctive chimney stack and roof extension which housed the bakery's canteen, and internally, a beautiful vaulted timber roof and stone staircase with balustrade.

61–63 Great Eastern Street, Shoreditch, EC2

In the nineteenth and twentieth centuries, the London furniture trade was centred in Shoreditch and crowded into small workshops and factories, where the stages of construction and finishing were carried out in different premises.

In 1890, 63 Great Eastern Street was occupied by Michael Hart, cabinet maker and from 1940 until 1968 by Natelys Ltd, rope, line and twine manufacturers. Then it became known as Valiant House and was occupied by Priestley & Moore, wholesale cutlery distributors until 1991. Salins Sundries Ltd, upholsterers' warehouse, occupied 61 Great Eastern Street from 1973 until 1976.

Former Queen Elizabeth Children's Hospital, Hackney Road, Bethnal Green, E2

In 1867, Quaker sisters, Ellen & Mary Elizabeth Phillips, established a Dispensary for Women & Children in two rented rooms in Virginia Road, Shoreditch. Ellen had worked in the cholera wards at the Royal London Hospital the previous year through a connection to Elizabeth Garrett Anderson, Britain's first qualified woman doctor.

By 1871, the sisters had the lease at 327 Hackney Road, on the site that became their custom-built hospital for sick children. Within three years, they laid the foundation stone for a building designed by William Beck in the adjoining Goldsmith's Row, attracting royal patronage and the support of Oscar Wilde who wrote a poem for their fund-raising. Terracotta sunflower friezes and details of iron-work and tiling reflected the Aesthetic Movement theme. In 1904, another building on Hackney Road was added, defining the triangular shape of the complex which continued to expand throughout the twentieth century.

Amalgamation with the Queen Elizabeth Children's Hospital of Shadwell in 1942 delivered the name by which it was most commonly known. Charles Dickens was patron of this organisation, which he discovered operating in a sail loft in 1869 and he raised money to build a dedicated hospital.

These two nineteenth century philanthropic ventures combined to create an institution that closed in 1996 when it was argued that the services were fulfilled elsewhere. Yet in 1974, this was the largest children's teaching hospital in Britain with three hundred students every year. Only the façade of the Hackney Road building still stands in the development of mostly luxury flats.

Holland House, 18–20 Deptford Bridge, Lewisham, SE8

Holland House was the premises of the Seager Gin Distillery. William Holland formed Holland & Co in the eighteen-fifties when he took over the distillery which had been established in the seventeen-seventies on the site of a former sugar refinery. Holland & Co sold out to Seager Evans in 1922 and gin production continued until Seager Evans were themselves taken over in 1956.

After plans for an art gallery were abandoned, Holland House is now serviced flats for short stays.

55 Pitfield Street, Hoxton, N1

This cinema designed by Lovegrove & Papworth was opened on 20th January 1914 and closed on 26th October 1956. Sold off by the Rank Organisation in June 1960, it became a meat packers, later a delicatessen warehouse and wholesaler, and then an artist's studio.

After lying empty for several years, a plan to reopen it as a community cinema was announced in 2004 and the auditorium was demolished in 2009 as part of this endeavour, which faltered leaving just the façade standing.

The façade was destroyed in 2016 and a replica constructed as part of a redevelopment combining a block of flats and a new cinema.

Former Unitarian Chapel, Stamford Street, Blackfriars, SE1

Designed in 1821 by Charles Parker, architect of Hoare's Bank in the Strand, the Chapel was demolished in the sixties apart from the portico and part of the ground floor, which stood in front of a car park for many years.

The Grade II listed Doric hexastyle portico has a triglyph frieze and a pediment over. Its central door has a shouldered architrave and iron gates. Each of the walls on either side has three blank windows with shouldered architraves.

The Antigallican, 155 Tooley Street, Bermondsey, SE1

The Anti-Gallican Society was founded around 1745 in response to the perceived cultural invasion of French culture and goods. The Society flourished in the Seven Years' War of 1756–1763 and the Napoleonic Wars of 1799–1805, persisting through the nineteenth century.

Dating from before 1822, this pub retained its xenophobic title until it closed in 2006, before succumbing to a nameless office development in 2011.

The Westminster Arms, 10 Praed Street, Paddington, W2

In Praed Street since before 1869, the Westminster Arms was façaded by the Hilton Metropole Hotel in 1989. Built of stuccoed brick, this Grade II listed façade consists of a pub frontage with pilasters and decorative ironwork, sash windows with architraves and cornices on the first floor and a cornice above.

The Spotted Dog, 38 High Road, Willesden, NW10

The Spotted Dog existed by 1762, and was described as 'a well accustomed Public House' in 1792. In the nineteenth century, it was famous for its pleasure gardens and in the nineteen-twenties it boasted a dance hall.

The White Hart, 121 Bishopsgate, EC2

'Its history as an inn can be of little less antiquity than that of the Tabard, the lodging house of the feast-loving Chaucer and the Canterbury pilgrims, or the Boar's Head in Eastcheap, the rendezvous of Prince Henry and his lewd companions,' wrote Charles Goss, Archivist at Bisopsgate Institute in 1930.

The White Hart was a coaching house and tavern dating from 1246, positioned on Bishopsgate just outside the gate of the City of London. Rebuilt in 1470 and 1827, it retained its medieval cellars and was constantly busy until it was bought by Sir Alan Sugar's company, Amsprop, in 2010 and reduced to a façade with a cylindrical office block on top, creating a monument to one man's ego.

The Duke of Cambridge, 25 Felix Street, Bethnal Green, E2

The earliest record of the Duke of Cambridge is when the land was purchased by William Brown in 1825 for £2,200, including the 'newly-erected tavern' which was 'being built in December 1823.' The Regent's Canal had just been cut through East London and, a quarter mile to the north, the Imperial Gas Works, powered by coal delivered by barge, opened in the same year. The Duke of Cambridge is one of the last vestiges from the early nineteenth century when the East End was transforming from a string of rural villages into an extended urban landscape.

I have chosen to conclude with a detailed analysis of the façading of the Duke of Cambridge which is the subject of the final photograph in my gallery of plates. I have done so, rather than pointing out what is wrong in every case illustrated, because I believe that this particular example incarnates all the problems inherent with façadism.

A CAUTIONARY TALE

It is rare that you cannot believe your eyes, yet such was my response when I first saw this chimera. When I examined the proposal for the façading of the Duke of Cambridge as part of the planning application for a larger housing development, I was astonished and appalled at how a new building appeared to have been forcibly inserted into an old building to create such a hybrid monster.

At the time, I dismissed it as a dystopian fiction because I could not believe it would ever get built, but the reality is so much worse than the proposal. Such is the ugly conflict between the old and the new, you can almost feel the humiliation and pain of the original building. The experience is akin to your dear old grandpa with the Father Christmas physique having his trousers stolen and you find him wandering bereft in the street, tricked out in a pair of garish Lycra shorts as the only option available.

It makes you wonder. How can anyone have thought that this treatment of a gracious nineteenth century pub was sympathetic? Or imagined that the finished result was acceptable as architecture? It stretches my imagination to grasp the aesthetic which permits an architect to arrive at such a disastrous compromise.

On his website, the architect describes it thus – 'A dynamic glazed box of 'Reglit' glass tubes juts out of the top of the brown and red brick façade of the original building, creating a relationship between old and new.' This statement set me thinking about the precise nature and quality of this relationship.

There are several ways in which the dominance of the new structure, crouching like an incubus on top of the old, expresses antipathy for the building it inhabits and denies the potential of any resolution of the diverse elements into a satisfactory architectural whole, which ought surely to be the object of the exercise.

Firstly, the scale, proportion, colour and idiosyncratic placement of the windows in the extension above ignore the form of those in the Duke of Cambridge, which now have clunky new frames inserted that differ significantly from the originals, dividing the windows in half laterally and compounding the inelegance of the configuration.

Secondly, the Reglit glass tubes with their strong vertical emphasis give the extension the effect of being extruded from the building below. The industrial modernity of these glass tubes is alien in this context, disregarding the traditional brickwork of the pub and preventing any integration of the different elements into a whole.

Thirdly, the former mansard roof of the Duke of Cambridge was raked, tilting away from the vertical walls beneath and held in place visually by the symmetrical flourishes of the Dutch gable on the front of the building, but the new extension does not resolve the form of the building below. Instead, by avoiding any acknowledgement of the Dutch gable, this crudely disproportionate rectangular box exists in conflict with the rest of the structure to discordant effect.

There is no reason why an architect could not use overtly modern materials in such a project, if the proportion and form of the building unified them within the design. Alternatively, I can see that by using traditional materials an architect could extend a building successfully in a form that contrasted with the pre-existing structure. The problem with the Duke of Cambridge is that the choice of form and the materials for the extension are both at odds with what is already there, and these deliberate decisions by the architect not to engage with the old building deliver an eyesore.

I feel disingenuous pointing this out because I expect architects to possess sensitivity for these essential concerns of their trade. I would like to imagine that the architect who chose to use the glass tubes on top of the Duke of Cambridge believed the luminosity of this material might impart a levity to the extension, as if it hovered above its predecessor like a cloud of light, or the beacon of a lighthouse. Even if this were the case, they have failed miserably for all the reasons outlined above.

In every example, it is paramount that attention be paid to any structure as an architectural whole, rather than simply sticking a new shed behind an old façade. Taking existing buildings and reworking them sympathetically to serve new purposes requires much more sophisticated thinking from architects and developers than is in evidence in the hideous structures which manifest this lamentable plague of façadism blighting our age.

The explanation of why the Duke of Cambridge has been degraded in this way lies with the two huge new buildings which are part of a larger development by the same architect and developer on the other side of Felix Street. Only one of these has yet been constructed and, out of a total of more than two hundred dwellings, it is intended that as few as 25% will be 'affordable.'

These vast irregularly shaped curved blocks possess no meaningful relationship in form or scale with the brick terraces of the Hackney Road or the dignified Guinness buildings constructed as social housing a century ago on the opposite side of Felix Street. Such is the generic nature of their design, they could equally be placed in Minneapolis or Milton Keynes because stylistically they do not belong anywhere, raising the suspicion that the form is dictated solely by an imperative to maximise volume and financial return rather than entertain any dialogue with the existing urban landscape. It is profoundly disappointing to witness how the current housing shortage has delivered a field day for exploitative development across the capital, rather than an incentive to address the real needs of Londoners.

Which brings me back to the Duke of Cambridge – because the anachronistic materials and forms which blight this formerly elegant structure, the Reglit glass tubes and the idiosyncratic window placing, are prominent features of the development across the road. In other words, the Duke of Cambridge has been adulterated in an attempt to unify it with the new housing blocks resulting in a dysfunctional conversation between two incompatible languages.

Although the Duke of Cambridge closed in 1998, people wanted to reopen it and give it new life, which would not have been impossible in this flourishing neighbourhood. An opportunity existed for the Duke of Cambridge to become the place where the residents of the Guinness buildings and the inhabitants of the new development could meet. But the opportunity of providing a social space for fellowship – as the pub had done for the previous one hundred and seventy-five years – was denied by the developer for the sake of cramming in a few more flats, thereby consigning it to the past. Retaining the lettering on the façade as a mere historic relic serves to remind us only of a life that has gone.

This loss raises the wider question of how the financial imperative driving such ill-conceived developments may be reconciled with our need for a city we want to live in and which serves the needs of all Londoners. The treatment of the Duke of Cambridge incarnates a metaphor of this conflict vividly and the ugliness of the outcome is a pertinent slap in the face, reminding us how blatantly any concern for quality of life or good architecture is being sacrificed for the sake of greed.

This disastrous hybrid is an unfortunate totem of where we are now, an object lesson for architectural students of what not to do, and we may be assured future generations will laugh in horror and derision at the folly of it. I have chosen to conclude my book with this abomination in Bethnal Green because I believe it is an all-time low.